D0433001

Cool Buildings

Contents

Mick Gowar
Character illustrations by Jon Stuart

OXFORD

What a view!

Billions of people live in cities around the world. Cities are full of amazing buildings. Buildings come in many different shapes and sizes. Look at all the buildings in this picture ...

A view of London.

Wow! What a great view!

So, what makes one building stand out from the rest? What makes a building *cool*?

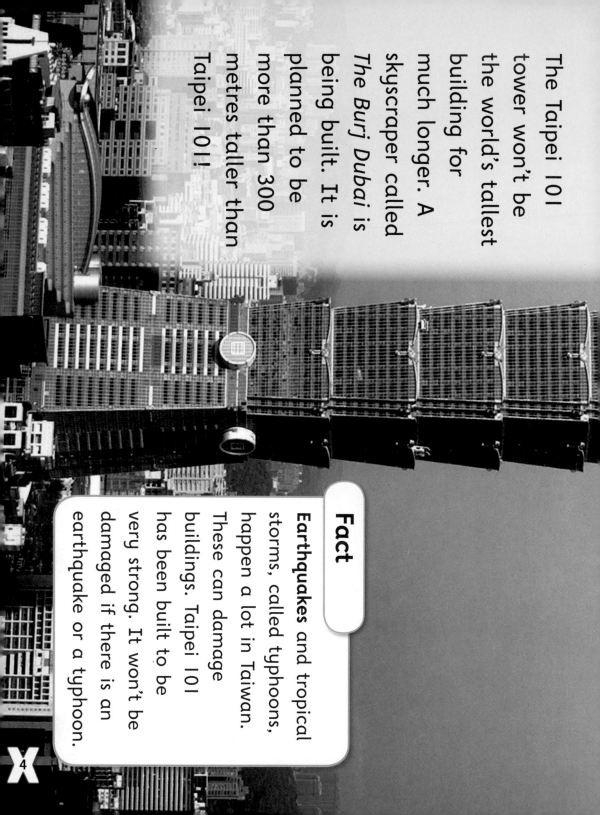

The Taipei 101 tower won't be the world's tallest building for much longer. A skyscraper called *The Burj Dubai* is being built. It is planned to be more than 300 metres taller than Taipei 101!

Fact

Earthquakes and tropical storms, called typhoons, happen a lot in Taiwan. These can damage buildings. Taipei 101 has been built to be very strong. It won't be damaged if there is an earthquake or a typhoon.

Size

This is the tallest building in the world. It is the *Taipei 101 tower*. It is a **skyscraper**. It is in the city of Taipei which is the largest city on the Island of Taiwan. It is 101 floors and is 508 metres high.

It's a long way down!

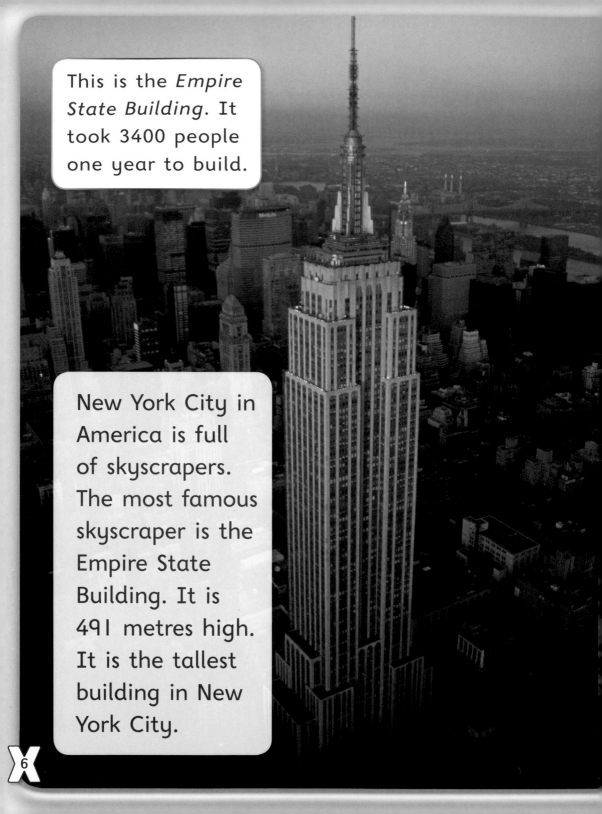

This is the *Empire State Building*. It took 3400 people one year to build.

New York City in America is full of skyscrapers. The most famous skyscraper is the Empire State Building. It is 491 metres high. It is the tallest building in New York City.

The Empire State Building has appeared in lots of films. One of the most famous films was *King Kong*. In the film, a giant ape called *Kong* climbs to the top of the building.

Shape

The Gherkin

I wonder why it's called the Gherkin?

One of the tallest buildings in London is *30 St Mary Axe*. It has 40 floors. From the top floor you can see the whole of London. It has been nicknamed the *Gherkin*.

The Gherkin looks curved but it is made from thousands of flat glass panels.

The Gherkin is a modern, environmentally friendly building. It takes half the power of a normal skyscraper to heat and light it.

Long ago, there was a library in the
Egyptian city of Alexandria. It was said
to contain every book that had ever been
written in Greek. 2000 years ago it was
destroyed in a fire.

Around the library is a big wall. It is carved with letters from every language in the world.

In 2002 a fabulous new library opened in Alexandria. It has space for 8 million books! It also contains 3 museums and 4 art galleries.

Materials

The O2 Arena.

Steel and Plastic

The *O2 Arena* in London is the biggest **dome** in the world. It is a huge plastic tent stretched between steel towers. It was first called the *Millennium Dome* because it opened in the year 2000. It contains an arena, restaurants and a music club.

This is the *Calico Bottle House* in the Mojave desert in California.

Glass

Buildings made of glass are common but this one is different. It is made out of thousands of glass bottles!

13

Ice

This must be one of the coolest buildings in the world. It's a hotel made of ice! Everything is made of ice – even the beds. If you stay there you need a special sleeping bag to keep you warm.

This ice hotel is near the city of Quebec in Canada.

This is not just cool, it's f...f...freezing!

Every year the ice hotel melts. So every year it has to be built again. There are 37 bedrooms in the hotel. It is made from about 500 tons of ice and 15 000 tons of snow! Every time it is built, it looks different!

Inside the ice hotel.

Old buildings like this need lots of repairs!

The *Tower of London* is one of the oldest buildings in Britain. It is over 900 years old. It has been a home for kings and queens, a fortress, an **armoury** and a prison.

The Tower of London is famous for its ravens.

Birds called ravens live at the tower. King John kept a small zoo in one of the towers. He kept lions, leopards and camels.

This is called the *Step Pyramid*. It's easy to see how it got its name!

Some of the oldest buildings in the world are the pyramids in Egypt. The Step Pyramid at Saqqara was one of the first large stone structures ever built.

The *Underwater Pyramid.*

Recently some **ruins** were discovered underwater, off the coast of Japan. Some people think they are the ruins of a pyramid. This pyramid is more than 5000 years older than the Step Pyramid in Egypt.

Other cool buildings

This is a real house. It is in the town of Sopot in Poland. It is called the *Crooked House*.

Is this a giant robot from outer space? No. It's a bank! It's the *Bank of Asia* in the city of Bangkok in Thailand.

This is a **factory** in Ohio in the USA. Can you guess what this factory makes?

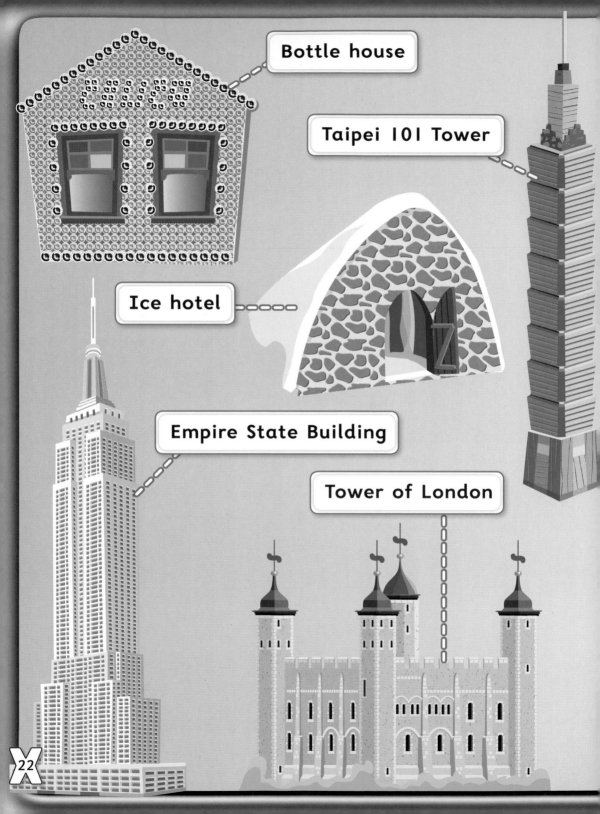

Bottle house

Taipei 101 Tower

Ice hotel

Empire State Building

Tower of London

22

Glossary

armoury   a place where weapons and suits of armour are kept

dome   a shape like the top half of a ball

earthquake   a time when the ground suddenly shakes. Strong earthquakes can destroy buildings

factory   a building where people make things with machines

ruin   a building that has fallen down

skyscraper   a very tall building

Index